Franklin D. Roosevelt

Judy Emerson
AR B.L.: 2.1
Points: 0.5

LG

First Biographies

Franklin D. Roosevelt

by Judy Emerson

Consulting Editor: Gail Saunders-Smith, Ph.D.
Consultant: James N. Druckman, Ph.D.
Assistant Professor of Political Science
University of Minnesota

Capstone
press
Mankato, Minnesota

Pebble Books are published by Capstone Press,
151 Good Counsel Drive, P.O. Box 669, Mankato, Minnesota 56002
www.capstonepress.com

1 2 3 4 5 6 09 08 07 06 05 04

Library of Congress Cataloging-in-Publication Data
Emerson, Judy.
    Franklin D. Roosevelt / by Judy Emerson.
    p. cm.—(First biographies)
    Summary: Simple text and photographs introduce the life of Franklin
Delano Roosevelt.
    Includes bibliographical references (p. 23) and index.
    ISBN-13: 978-0-7368-2087-5 (hardcover)
    ISBN-10: 0-7368-2087-6 (hardcover)
    ISBN-13: 978-0-7368-5084-1 (paperback)
    ISBN-10: 0-7368-5084-8 (paperback)
    1. Roosevelt, Franklin D. (Franklin Delano), 1882–1945—Juvenile literature.
2. Presidents—United States—Biography—Juvenile literature. [1. Roosevelt,
Franklin D. (Franklin Delano), 1882–1945. 2. Presidents.] I. Title. II. Series: First
biographies (Mankato, Minn.)
E807.E56 2004
973.917′092—dc22   2003015250

Note to Parents and Teachers

The First Biographies series supports national history standards for
units on people and culture. This book describes and illustrates the
life of Franklin D. Roosevelt. The photographs support early readers
in understanding the text. This book also introduces early readers to
subject-specific vocabulary words, which are defined in the
Glossary. Early readers may need assistance to read some words
and to use the Table of Contents, Glossary, Read More, Internet
Sites, and Index/Word List sections of the book.

Table of Contents

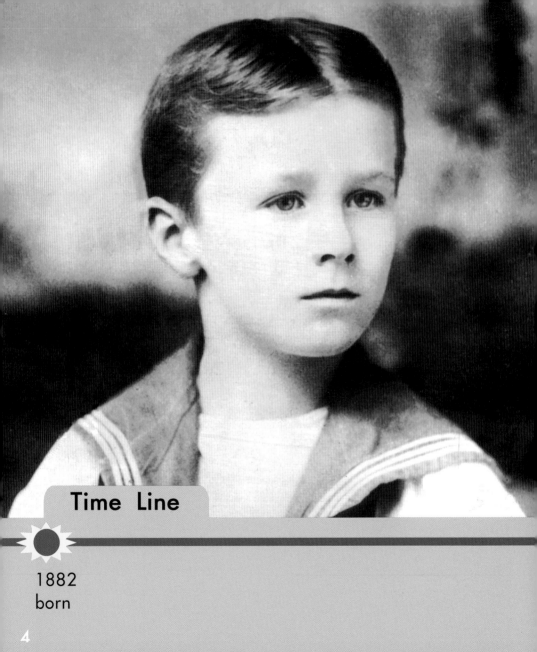

Time Line

1882
born

Franklin D. Roosevelt

Franklin Delano Roosevelt was born in 1882 in New York. His family was rich. Tutors helped Franklin with his schoolwork. Nannies helped take care of him.

 Franklin at age 7

1882
born

1903
graduates
from Harvard

Franklin went to Harvard University. He studied and played football. Franklin graduated in 1903. He later went to Columbia Law School.

 Franklin in 1903

Time Line

1882	1903	1905
born	graduates from Harvard	marries Eleanor Roosevelt

Early Years

Franklin married Eleanor Roosevelt in 1905. They were distant cousins. Franklin and Eleanor had six children.

Eleanor and Franklin during their honeymoon in Italy

Time Line

| 1882 born | 1903 graduates from Harvard | 1905 marries Eleanor Roosevelt | 1910 elected to NY State Senate |

Franklin was elected to the New York State Senate in 1910. He later worked as the assistant secretary of the U.S. Navy. In 1928, he was elected governor of New York.

Franklin as assistant secretary of the U.S. Navy in 1913

Time Line

1882 born	**1903** graduates from Harvard	**1905** marries Eleanor Roosevelt	**1910** elected to NY State Senate

In 1921, Franklin became sick with polio. He could not walk without help. He walked with crutches or had someone help him. He later used a wheelchair.

Franklin using crutches in 1926

1921
became sick
with polio

Time Line

| 1882 born | 1903 graduates from Harvard | 1905 marries Eleanor Roosevelt | 1910 elected to NY State Senate |

President Roosevelt

Franklin became president in 1933. Many Americans did not have jobs, food, or homes. This time was called the Great Depression. Franklin wanted to help.

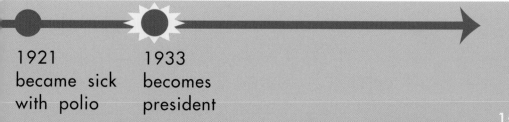

1921
became sick
with polio

1933
becomes
president

Time Line

1882	1903	1905	1910
born	graduates from Harvard	marries Eleanor Roosevelt	elected to NY State Senate

Working with Congress, Franklin created programs and jobs to help Americans. He called these plans the "New Deal." Franklin told Americans about his ideas on the radio.

1921
became sick
with polio

1933
becomes
president

Time Line

1882
born

1903
graduates
from Harvard

1905
marries
Eleanor Roosevelt

1910
elected to NY
State Senate

World War II started
in 1939. Two years
later, the United States
joined the war. Franklin
and other Americans worked
hard to help win the war.

American soldiers in France in 1944

1921
became sick
with polio

1933
becomes
president

1939
World War II
begins

Time Line

1882	1903	1905	1910
born	graduates from Harvard	marries Eleanor Roosevelt	elected to NY State Senate

Remembering Franklin

Franklin Roosevelt died in 1945. He had been elected president four times. People remember him as a president who helped people through hard times.

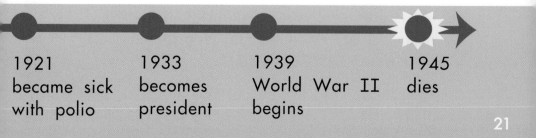

1921
became sick
with polio

1933
becomes
president

1939
World War II
begins

1945
dies

Glossary

Great Depression—a period of time in the United States when many people lost their jobs; the Great Depression was from 1929 to 1939.

nanny—someone who is trained to take care of young children in the children's homes

New Deal—programs and policies Franklin helped create in the 1930s to help the United States during the Great Depression

polio—a disease that attacks the nerves, spinal cord, and brain; people with polio are often unable to move.

tutor—a teacher who gives lessons to only one student or a small group of students

World War II—a war in which the United States, France, Great Britain, the Soviet Union and other countries defeated Germany, Italy, and Japan; World War II lasted from 1939 to 1945.

Read More

Joseph, Paul. *Franklin D. Roosevelt.* United States Presidents. Minneapolis: Abdo, 2002.

Knapp, Ron. *Franklin D. Roosevelt.* Presidents. Berkeley Heights, N.J.: MyReportLinks.com Books, 2002.

Maupin, Melissa. *Franklin D. Roosevelt: Our Thirty-Second President.* Chanhassen, Minn.: Child's World, 2002.

Internet Sites

FactHound offers a safe, fun way to find Internet sites related to this book. All of the sites on FactHound have been researched by our staff.

Here's how:

1. Visit *www.facthound.com*
2. Type in this special code **0736820876** for age-appropriate sites. Or enter a search word related to this book for a more general search.
3. Click on the **Fetch It** button.

FactHound will fetch the best sites for you!

Index/Word List

Word Count: 223
Early-Intervention Level: 20

Editorial Credits

Mari C. Schuh, editor; Heather Kindseth, cover designer and illustrator; Enoch Peterson, production designer; Scott Thoms, photo researcher; Karen Risch, product planning editor

Photo Credits

Corbis, 8; Bettmann, 12, 18

Getty Images/Hulton Archive, cover, 1, 4, 10, 14, 20

Stock Montage Inc., 6, 16